The Lightning ScoreBook

Dr. Bo Wagner

Word of His Mouth Publisher
Mooresboro, NC

All Scripture quotations are taken from the **King James Version** of the Bible.

ISBN: 978-0-9856042-0-2
Printed in the United States of America
© 2012 Dr. Bo Wagner (Robert Arthur Wagner)

Word of His Mouth Publishers
PO Box 256
Mooresboro, NC 28114

To order more copies of this book please call 704-477-5439 or visit our web page at www.wordofhismouth.com.

L	Living
I	In
G	God's
H	Holy
T	Truth
N	New
I	Identity
N	New
G	Goals

Name _____

Lightning Year _____

Church _____

Team Name _____

Table of Content

Notes

Please, write any special notes that your Youth Leaders tell you are things you will need to know.

_____
_____
_____
_____
_____
_____
_____
_____
_____
_____
_____
_____
_____
_____
_____
_____
_____
_____
_____
_____
_____
_____
_____
_____
_____
_____
_____
_____
_____
_____
_____

General Verse List

Verses have to be said perfectly (you cannot miss any words). You have only two opportunities to say each verse. Once you have said the verse correctly the first time, have your sponsor initial the first column.

Once you say a verse during the year, keep it memorized! You will have an opportunity to say it again on week 34 for even more points! (You can't say it on week 34 unless you have said it the first time before that day.) Once you have said your verse on week 34 have your sponsor initial the second column.

Note to Sponsor: Once a young person has tried to say a verse twice without saying it correctly, please, cross the verse out so they can not try it again this year.

Points for verses:
First time:... 1,000 points
Second time on week 34:.......................................3,000 points

	First Time	Week 34
Genesis 1:1		
Leviticus 19:16		
Numbers 32:23		
Deuteronomy 22:5		
Joshua 1:8		
Joshua 24:15		
Psalm 1:1		
Psalm 1:2		
Psalm 1:3		
Psalm 1:4		
Psalm 1:5		
Psalm 1:6		

Psalm 5:11   _____   _____
Psalm 23:1   _____   _____
Psalm 23:2   _____   _____
Psalm 23:3   _____   _____
Psalm 23:4   _____   _____
Psalm 23:5   _____   _____
Psalm 23:6   _____   _____
Psalm 51:10   _____   _____
Psalm 66:18   _____   _____
Psalm 100:1   _____   _____
Psalm 100:2   _____   _____
Psalm 100:3   _____   _____
Psalm 100:4   _____   _____
Psalm 100:5   _____   _____
Psalm 101:3   _____   _____
Psalm 119:1   _____   _____
Psalm 119:2   _____   _____
Psalm 119:3   _____   _____
Psalm 119:4   _____   _____
Psalm 119:5   _____   _____
Psalm 119:6   _____   _____
Psalm 119:7   _____   _____
Psalm 119:8   _____   _____
Psalm 119:9   _____   _____
Psalm 119:10   _____   _____
Psalm 119:11   _____   _____
Psalm 119:12   _____   _____
Psalm 119:13   _____   _____
Psalm 119:14   _____   _____
Psalm 119:15   _____   _____
Psalm 119:16   _____   _____
Psalm 119:17   _____   _____
Psalm 119:18   _____   _____
Psalm 119:19   _____   _____
Psalm 119:20   _____   _____
Psalm 119:21   _____   _____
Psalm 119:22   _____   _____

Psalm 119:23 _____ _____
Psalm 119:24 _____ _____
Psalm 119:25 _____ _____
Psalm 119:26 _____ _____
Psalm 119:27 _____ _____
Psalm 119:28 _____ _____
Psalm 119:29 _____ _____
Psalm 119:30 _____ _____
Psalm 119:31 _____ _____
Psalm 119:32 _____ _____
Psalm 119:33 _____ _____
Psalm 119:34 _____ _____
Psalm 119:35 _____ _____
Psalm 119:36 _____ _____
Psalm 119:37 _____ _____
Psalm 119:38 _____ _____
Psalm 119:39 _____ _____
Psalm 119:40 _____ _____
Psalm 119:41 _____ _____
Psalm 119:42 _____ _____
Psalm 119:43 _____ _____
Psalm 119:44 _____ _____
Psalm 119:45 _____ _____
Psalm 119:46 _____ _____
Psalm 119:47 _____ _____
Psalm 119:48 _____ _____
Psalm 119:49 _____ _____
Psalm 119:50 _____ _____
Psalm 119:51 _____ _____
Psalm 119:52 _____ _____
Psalm 119:53 _____ _____
Psalm 119:54 _____ _____
Psalm 119:55 _____ _____
Psalm 119:56 _____ _____
Psalm 119:57 _____ _____
Psalm 119:58 _____ _____
Psalm 119:59 _____ _____

Psalm 119:60 _____ _____
Psalm 119:61 _____ _____
Psalm 119:62 _____ _____
Psalm 119:63 _____ _____
Psalm 119:64 _____ _____
Psalm 119:65 _____ _____
Psalm 119:66 _____ _____
Psalm 119:67 _____ _____
Psalm 119:68 _____ _____
Psalm 119:69 _____ _____
Psalm 119:70 _____ _____
Psalm 119:71 _____ _____
Psalm 119:72 _____ _____
Psalm 119:73 _____ _____
Psalm 119:74 _____ _____
Psalm 119:75 _____ _____
Psalm 119:76 _____ _____
Psalm 119:77 _____ _____
Psalm 119:78 _____ _____
Psalm 119:79 _____ _____
Psalm 119:80 _____ _____
Psalm 119:81 _____ _____
Psalm 119:82 _____ _____
Psalm 119:83 _____ _____
Psalm 119:84 _____ _____
Psalm 119:85 _____ _____
Psalm 119:86 _____ _____
Psalm 119:87 _____ _____
Psalm 119:88 _____ _____
Psalm 119:89 _____ _____
Psalm 119:90 _____ _____
Psalm 119:91 _____ _____
Psalm 119:92 _____ _____
Psalm 119:93 _____ _____
Psalm 119:94 _____ _____
Psalm 119:95 _____ _____
Psalm 119:96 _____ _____

Psalm 119:97 _____ _____
Psalm 119:98 _____ _____
Psalm 119:99 _____ _____
Psalm 119:100 _____ _____
Psalm 119:101 _____ _____
Psalm 119:102 _____ _____
Psalm 119:103 _____ _____
Psalm 119:104 _____ _____
Psalm 119:105 _____ _____
Psalm 119:106 _____ _____
Psalm 119:107 _____ _____
Psalm 119:108 _____ _____
Psalm 119:109 _____ _____
Psalm 119:110 _____ _____
Psalm 119:111 _____ _____
Psalm 119:112 _____ _____
Psalm 119:113 _____ _____
Psalm 119:114 _____ _____
Psalm 119:115 _____ _____
Psalm 119:116 _____ _____
Psalm 119:117 _____ _____
Psalm 119:118 _____ _____
Psalm 119:119 _____ _____
Psalm 119:120 _____ _____
Psalm 119:121 _____ _____
Psalm 119:122 _____ _____
Psalm 119:123 _____ _____
Psalm 119:124 _____ _____
Psalm 119:125 _____ _____
Psalm 119:126 _____ _____
Psalm 119:127 _____ _____
Psalm 119:128 _____ _____
Psalm 119:129 _____ _____
Psalm 119:130 _____ _____
Psalm 119:131 _____ _____
Psalm 119:132 _____ _____
Psalm 119:133 _____ _____

Psalm 119:134 _____ _____
Psalm 119:135 _____ _____
Psalm 119:136 _____ _____
Psalm 119:137 _____ _____
Psalm 119:138 _____ _____
Psalm 119:139 _____ _____
Psalm 119:140 _____ _____
Psalm 119:141 _____ _____
Psalm 119:142 _____ _____
Psalm 119:143 _____ _____
Psalm 119:144 _____ _____
Psalm 119:145 _____ _____
Psalm 119:146 _____ _____
Psalm 119:147 _____ _____
Psalm 119:148 _____ _____
Psalm 119:149 _____ _____
Psalm 119:150 _____ _____
Psalm 119:151 _____ _____
Psalm 119:152 _____ _____
Psalm 119:153 _____ _____
Psalm 119:154 _____ _____
Psalm 119:155 _____ _____
Psalm 119:156 _____ _____
Psalm 119:157 _____ _____
Psalm 119:158 _____ _____
Psalm 119:159 _____ _____
Psalm 119:160 _____ _____
Psalm 119:161 _____ _____
Psalm 119:162 _____ _____
Psalm 119:163 _____ _____
Psalm 119:164 _____ _____
Psalm 119:165 _____ _____
Psalm 119:166 _____ _____
Psalm 119:167 _____ _____
Psalm 119:168 _____ _____
Psalm 119:169 _____ _____
Psalm 119:170 _____ _____

Psalm 119:171 _____ _____
Psalm 119:172 _____ _____
Psalm 119:173 _____ _____
Psalm 119:174 _____ _____
Psalm 119:175 _____ _____
Psalm 119:176 _____ _____
Psalm 122:1 _____ _____
Psalm 141:3 _____ _____
Proverbs 1:10 _____ _____
Proverbs 3:5 _____ _____
Proverbs 3:6 _____ _____
Proverbs 3:9 _____ _____
Proverbs 3:10 _____ _____
Proverbs 15:1 _____ _____
Proverbs 22:1 _____ _____
Proverbs 22:4 _____ _____
Proverbs 22:6 _____ _____
Proverbs 22:7 _____ _____
Proverbs 26:20 _____ _____
Proverbs 31:10 _____ _____
Proverbs 31:26 _____ _____
Isaiah 26:3 _____ _____
Isaiah 40:31 _____ _____
Isaiah 55:6 _____ _____
Isaiah 53:1 _____ _____
Isaiah 53:2 _____ _____
Isaiah 53:3 _____ _____
Isaiah 53:4 _____ _____
Isaiah 53:5 _____ _____
Isaiah 53:6 _____ _____
Isaiah 53:7 _____ _____
Isaiah 53:8 _____ _____
Isaiah 53:9 _____ _____
Isaiah 53:10 _____ _____
Isaiah 53:11 _____ _____
Isaiah 53:12 _____ _____
Isaiah 64:6 _____ _____

Lamentations 3:22 _____ _____
Lamentations 3:23 _____ _____
Daniel 1:8 _____ _____
Amos 3:3 _____ _____
Malachi 3:8 _____ _____
Malachi 3:9 _____ _____
Malachi 3:10 _____ _____
Matthew 6:33 _____ _____
Matthew 28:18 _____ _____
Matthew 28:19 _____ _____
Matthew 28:20 _____ _____
Mark 16:15 _____ _____
Luke 16:19 _____ _____
Luke 16:20 _____ _____
Luke 16:21 _____ _____
Luke 16:22 _____ _____
Luke 16:23 _____ _____
Luke 16:24 _____ _____
Luke 16:25 _____ _____
Luke 16:26 _____ _____
Luke 16:27 _____ _____
Luke 16:28 _____ _____
Luke 16:29 _____ _____
Luke 16:30 _____ _____
Luke 16:31 _____ _____
John 3:1 _____ _____
John 3:2 _____ _____
John 3:3 _____ _____
John 3:4 _____ _____
John 3:5 _____ _____
John 3:6 _____ _____
John 3:7 _____ _____
John 3:8 _____ _____
John 3:9 _____ _____
John 3:10 _____ _____
John 3:11 _____ _____
John 3:12 _____ _____

John 3:13	_____	_____
John 3:14	_____	_____
John 3:15	_____	_____
John 3:16	_____	_____
John 3:17	_____	_____
John 11:35	_____	_____
John 14:6	_____	_____
Acts 1:8	_____	_____
Acts 20:28	_____	_____
1 Corinthians 7:1	_____	_____
1 Corinthians 16:1	_____	_____
2 Corinthians 6:17	_____	_____
2 Corinthians 6:18	_____	_____
Galatians 6:7	_____	_____
Galatians 6:8	_____	_____
Ephesians 4:29	_____	_____
Ephesians 4:30	_____	_____
Ephesians 4:31	_____	_____
Ephesians 4:32	_____	_____
Ephesians 5:21	_____	_____
Ephesians 5:22	_____	_____
Ephesians 5:23	_____	_____
Ephesians 5:24	_____	_____
Ephesians 5:25	_____	_____
Ephesians 6:1	_____	_____
Philippians 2:14	_____	_____
Philippians 4:13	_____	_____
Philippians 4:19	_____	_____
Colossians 4:6	_____	_____
1 Thessalonians 4:13	_____	_____
1 Thessalonians 4:14	_____	_____
1 Thessalonians 4:15	_____	_____
1 Thessalonians 4:16	_____	_____
1 Thessalonians 4:17	_____	_____
1 Thessalonians 4:18	_____	_____
1 Timothy 2:9	_____	_____
1 Timothy 5:17	_____	_____

Titus 3:5 _____ _____
Hebrews 4:16 _____ _____
Hebrews 11:6 _____ _____
Hebrews 12:1 _____ _____
Hebrews 12:2 _____ _____
Hebrews 13:8 _____ _____
Hebrews 13:17 _____ _____
James 1:5 _____ _____
James 1:12 _____ _____
James 1:22 _____ _____
James 4:7 _____ _____
James 4:8 _____ _____
James 4:10 _____ _____
James 4:14 _____ _____
1 Peter 5:8 _____ _____
1 John 1:7 _____ _____
1 John 1:9 _____ _____
1 John 2:1 _____ _____
1 John 2:2 _____ _____
1 John 2:15 _____ _____
1 John 2:16 _____ _____
1 John 2:17 _____ _____
Revelation 3:20 _____ _____
Revelation 4:11 _____ _____

Gold Verses

You must quote the gold verses perfectly. (You can not miss any words.) You must also quote the meaning of these verses. You may say them one time during the year. These verses are required to go on certain trips and activities! Have your sponsor initial the blank when said perfectly. (You only get two tries!)

Note to Sponsor: Once a young person has tried to say a verse twice without saying it correctly, please, cross the verse out so they can not try it again this year.

Points for verses with meaning . . . . 3,000 points

_____ **A - 1 Thessalonians 5:22 Abstain from all appearance of evil.**
Basic meaning: Not only should we stay away from things that are wrong, we are to stay away from everything that would look wrong. Our testimony is too valuable to treat lightly!

_____ **B - Galatians 6:7 Be not deceived; God is not mocked: for whatsoever a man soweth, that shall he also reap.**
Basic meaning: All of your actions have consequences.

_____ **C - 1 Peter 5:7 Casting all your care upon him; for he careth for you.**
Basic meaning: God cares about your every worry or hurt. So do not "lay" your burdens on Him where you are close enough to pick them right back up, "cast" them on Him!

_____ **D - 1 Corinthians 11:14 Doth not even nature itself teach you, that, if a man have long hair, it is a shame unto him?**

Basic meaning: This verse is not talking about "nature" in the sense of "the animal kingdom". It means that everyone understands naturally that long hair is not normal on a man. No guy every decided to "rebel" by getting a "preacher-cut!"

_____ **E - James 1:17 Every good gift and every perfect gift is from above, and cometh down from the Father of lights, with whom is no variableness, neither shadow of turning.**

Basic meaning: We have no reason to brag about anything, because anything good about us (athletic ability, good looks, wealth, etc.) is a gift from God. He is the Father of lights, meaning that He created the light. He has no variableness, which means that He is utterly consistent. He is so unchanging, even His shadow does not waver.

_____ **F - Ephesians 2:8 For by grace are ye saved through faith; and that not of yourselves: *it is* the gift of God: 9 Not of works, lest any man should boast.**

Basic meaning: No one is ever saved by works (like baptism, church membership, keeping the Ten Commandments, etc.). We are only saved through grace. Grace means "unmerited favor, a free gift." Even the faith that we believe on Him with is part of the gift of grace! Getting saved is not of works, staying saved is not of works, so no man can ever brag about it. Also, the English words "are ye saved" is one word in Greek, and it is in the perfect tense, meaning that it can never ever be undone. We call that Eternal Security.

_____ **G - Matthew 28:19 Go ye therefore, and teach all nations, baptizing them in the name of the Father, and of the Son, and of the Holy Ghost: 20 Teaching them to observe all things whatsoever I have commanded you: and, lo, I am with you alway,** _even_ **unto the end of the world. Amen.**

Basic meaning: This passage is called "The Great Commission." This is what God expects from believers, from the church. There are three parts to it. We are to win people to the Lord, baptized them, and teaching them what the Bible says.

_____ **H - Matthew 24:35 Heaven and earth shall pass away, but my words shall not pass away.**

Basic meaning: This verse teaches the preservation of Scripture. There are no "missing parts" of Scripture, every book, chapter, verse, and word that God wanted in it was in it from the time it was first written, is still in it today and will be in it for all time and eternity. You can trust every single word of your Bible!

_____ **I - Psalm 101:3 I will set no wicked thing before mine eyes: I hate the work of them that turn aside;** _it_ **shall not cleave to me.**

Basic meaning: Never look at wicked things (Pornography, bad movies or bad tv shows). If you do, those things will stick to your mind and heart!

_____ **J - John 14:6 Jesus saith unto him, I am the way, the truth, and the life: no man cometh unto the Father, but by me.**

Basic meaning: Jesus is the only way of salvation. You cannot be saved through Muhammad or Buddha or the pope or anyone else, only through Jesus.

_____ **K - Proverbs 4:23 Keep thy heart with all diligence; for out of it** _are_ **the issues of life.**

Basic meaning: Put a guard around your heart, never allowing any evil influences into it. What goes into your heart will affect every issue of your life. The verses around this one tell you how to guard your heart: be careful what you hear, be careful what you see, be careful where you go, and be careful what decisions you make.

_____ **L - Philippians 2:5 Let this mind be in you, which was also in Christ Jesus: 6 Who, being in the form of God, thought it not robbery to be equal with God: 7 But made himself of no reputation, and took upon him the form of a servant, and was made in the likeness of men: 8 And being found in fashion as a man, he humbled himself, and became obedient unto death, even the death of the cross.**
Basis meaning: Think like Jesus thinks. Jesus, who was God, still did not try to "make a reputation" for Himself. Jesus was a servant. Jesus humbled Himself, and was obedient even to the point of dying on the cross. So in basic form, thinking like Jesus means being humble and never self-centered.

_____ **M - Hebrews 13:4 Marriage *is* honourable in all, and the bed undefiled: but whoremongers and adulterers God will judge.**
Basic meaning: Marriage, the union of one man and one woman for life, is honorable and sexual relations in that marriage is pure in the sight of God. But those who in any way engage in any form of sex before marriage or outside of marriage God will judge.

_____ **N - Hebrews 10:25 Not forsaking the assembling of ourselves together, as the manner of some *is*; but exhorting *one another*: and so much the more, as ye see the day approaching.**
Basic meaning: Don't lay out of church. Some do, but

you shouldn't. You should be there to encourage one another, especially since we can see the day of the Lord's return approaching.

_____ **O - Proverbs 13:10 Only by pride cometh contention: but with the well advised *is* wisdom.**
Basic meaning: Any time there is contention, fighting and arguing, pride is always the root cause.

_____ **P - 1 Thessalonians 5:21 Prove all things; hold fast that which is good.**
Basic meaning: Put everything to the test, whether it be belief or behavior. Compare it to the measuring stick, the written Word of God. If the Bible does not vouch for it, get rid of it!

_____ **Q - 1 Thessalonians 5:19 Quench not the Spirit.**
Basic meaning: The Holy Spirit, a real person, wants to burn like a fire in your life. He wants to make things exciting and powerful. He wants to move you and lead you. Don't pour water on that fire!

_____ **R - Proverbs 14:34 Righteousness exalteth a nation: but sin *is* a reproach to any people.**
Basic meaning: It is not money or geography or military might that makes a nation great. It is righteousness that makes a nation great. And any nation, no matter how big, strong, or wealthy, will eventually pay the price for sin.

_____ **S - 2 Timothy 2:15 Study to shew thyself approved unto God, a workman that needeth not to be ashamed, rightly dividing the word of truth.**
Basic meaning: We are supposed to study, and this especially means to study the Bible. Don't just read it, study it! We are spiritual workmen, and if we do not study, we will end up embarrassed and ashamed,

because we will not know how to "rightly divide" the Bible. For instance, Christ has fulfilled the Old Testament ceremonial law with His sacrifice on Calvary. We do not need to sacrifice lambs anymore. That is "rightly dividing" the word of truth.

_____ **T - Leviticus 18:22 Thou shalt not lie with mankind, as with womankind: it *is* abomination.**
Basic meaning: God regards as disgusting and filthy any form of homosexuality or lesbianism. It is not an "alternate lifestyle," it is an abomination!

_____ **U - 1 Peter 4:9 Use hospitality one to another without grudging.**
Basic meaning: Don't just extend hospitality to your Christian brothers and sisters, do so gladly.

_____ **V - John 5:24 Verily, verily, I say unto you, He that heareth my word, and believeth on him that sent me, hath everlasting life, and shall not come into condemnation; but is passed from death unto life.**
Basic meaning: If you have heard the Word of God, and then truly believed on Jesus, you have everlasting life. You are not ever going to go to Hell. You have already passed from death unto life. This is another among many verses that clearly teach eternal security.

_____ **W - Proverbs 20:1 Wine *is* a mocker, strong drink *is* raging: and whosoever is deceived thereby is not wise.**
Basic meaning: Anyone who puts any alcoholic beverage to their lips is a fool.

_____ **X - John 3:3b ... Except a man be born again, he cannot see the kingdom of God.**
Basic meaning: No one gets to Heaven without getting saved. No one is born saved. No baby can "have their

original sin washed away." A person must recognize himself as a sinner, repent, and undergo the new birth of salvation.

_____ **Y - Leviticus 19:11 Ye shall not steal, neither deal falsely, neither lie one to another.**
Basic meaning: Don't steal (that one is obvious). Don't lie (that one is also obvious). Don't deal falsely. (Not so obvious!) That phrase means "don't find a way to deceive someone without actually lying." In other words, a scam in which you make someone believe a lie that you lead them into is just as bad as if you had actually said the lie.

_____ **Z - Isaiah 1:27 Zion shall be redeemed with judgment, and her converts with righteousness.**
Basic meaning: God is not done with the Jews. He will redeem them and re-build them as a people. Every promise that he made to them, including the promise of an earthly kingdom, will come to pass.

Sliding Safely Home Verses

You must quote the verse perfectly along with the meaning. These verses are ones that will help you hit the ball as you become a tccn, round third as your teen years pass by, and slide safely home into adulthood!

Have your sponsor initial the blank when you have said your verse. (You only get two tries, so practice hard!)

Note to Sponsor: Once a young person has tried to say a verse twice without saying it correctly, please, cross the verse out so they can not try it again this year.

Points for verse with meaning . . . . 3,000 points

_____ **Proverbs 1:8 My son, hear the instruction of thy father, and forsake not the law of thy mother:**
Basic Meaning: Don't be like most foolish teenagers; don't get to the point where you will not immediately obey your mom and dad.

_____ **Hebrews 13:7 Remember them which have the rule over you, who have spoken unto you the word of God: whose faith follow, considering the end of *their* conversation.**
Basic meaning: Obey your pastor. He should be able to tell you something and have you obey with no argument.

_____ **2 Corinthians 6:14 Be ye not unequally yoked together with unbelievers: for what fellowship hath righteousness with unrighteousness? and what communion hath light with darkness?**

Basic meaning: You are never, EVER to date or marry an unsaved person!

_____ **Psalm 1:1 Blessed** *is* **the man that walketh not in the counsel of the ungodly, nor standeth in the way of sinners, nor sitteth in the seat of the scornful. 2 But his delight** *is* **in the law of the LORD; and in his law doth he meditate day and night. 3 And he shall be like a tree planted by the rivers of water, that bringeth forth his fruit in his season; his leaf also shall not wither; and whatsoever he doeth shall prosper.**
Basic meaning: Don't hang around sinful people. Don't go where they go, don't do what they do. Your friends will determine your future.

_____ **John 3:19 And this is the condemnation, that light is come into the world, and men loved darkness rather than light, because their deeds were evil.**
Basic meaning: Don't do or say anything that you feel like you have to hide from parents or pastor (things like bad pictures and evil conversations online or by text!) If you have to hide it, it is wrong.

_____ **1 Corinthians 7:1 Now concerning the things whereof ye wrote unto me:** *It is* **good for a man not to touch a woman.**
Basic meaning: Keep your hands, lips, and everything else off of people until you get married!

_____ **Leviticus 19:32 Thou shalt rise up before the hoary head, and honour the face of the old man, and fear thy God: I am the LORD.**
Basic meaning: Respect and honor adults!

_____ **Ephesians 4:29 Let no corrupt communication proceed out of your mouth, but that which is good**

to the use of edifying, that it may minister grace unto the hearers.
Basic meaning: Never ever cuss or talk dirty.

_____ **Nehemiah 10:39b ...and we will not forsake the house of our God.**
Basic meaning: Never lay out of church.

_____ **Proverbs 20:1 Wine *is* a mocker, strong drink *is* raging: and whosoever is deceived thereby is not wise.**
Basic meaning: Anyone who puts any alcoholic beverage to their lips is a fool, so don't do it!

_____ **1 Corinthians 6:19 What? know ye not that your body is the temple of the Holy Ghost *which is* in you, which ye have of God, and ye are not your own? 20 For ye are bought with a price: therefore glorify God in your body, and in your spirit, which are God's.**
Basic meaning: Among other things, this verse teaches you to never do drugs. Your body belongs to God, and you are therefore not to put things into your body to ruin it.

_____ **Leviticus 19:28 Ye shall not make any cuttings in your flesh for the dead, nor print any marks upon you: I am the Lord.**
Basic meaning: You cannot get any tattoos.

_____ **Romans 12:2 And be not conformed to this world: but be ye transformed by the renewing of your mind, that ye may prove what is that good, and acceptable, and perfect, will of God.**
Basic meaning: Don't do anything to make yourself look like popular worldly people (i.e. body piercings,

weird hairdos, etc.) always determine to be godly and
to look godly.

Leading Someone to Christ Verse List

Verses have to be said perfectly (you cannot miss any words). You have only two opportunities to say each verse. Once you have said the verse correctly, have your sponsor initial the blank.

Note to Sponsor: Once a young person has tried to say a verse twice without saying it correctly, please, cross the verse out so they can not try it again this year.

Points for verses .... 1,000 points

_____ **Romans 3:10   As it is written, There is none righteous, no, not one:**

_____ **Romans 3:23 For all have sinned, and come short of the glory of God;**

_____ **Romans 6:23 For the wages of sin *is* death; but the gift of God *is* eternal life through Jesus Christ our Lord.**

_____ **Romans 5:8 But God commendeth his love toward us, in that, while we were yet sinners, Christ died for us.**

_____ **Luke 13:3 I tell you, Nay: but, except ye repent, ye shall all likewise perish.**

_____ **Luke 13:5 I tell you, Nay: but, except ye repent, ye shall all likewise perish.**

_____ **Romans 10:9 That if thou shalt confess with thy mouth the Lord Jesus, and shalt believe in thine heart that God hath raised him from the dead, thou shalt be saved.**

_____ **Romans 10:13 For whosoever shall call upon the name of the Lord shall be saved.**

Church Etiquette Memory Section

Points for Verse . . . . 1,000 points
Points for Rules . . . . 1,000 points each for rule

_____ **1 Timothy 3:15 But if I tarry long, that thou mayest know how thou oughtest to behave thyself in the house of God, which is the church of the living God, the pillar and ground of the truth.**

Much of what Paul wrote, and other Bible writers as well, was to tell us how to behave in church. Here are some of the church behavior principles we expect for you to follow:

_____ 1. Dress your best for church.
_____ 2. Do not engage in "PC" in church (PC: Physical Contact with the opposite sex!)
_____ 3. Do not engage in "electronic distractions" in church. You are here to worship God!
_____ 4. Sit up straight. There are no lounge chairs in here.
_____ 5. Get over yourself. Church is not about you.
_____ 6. Do not sit in the back unless your parents are back there.
_____ 7. Respect your pastor and have his back!
_____ 8. Do not put gum or candy anywhere but your mouth or a trash can.
_____ 9. Take care of the House of God; keep it and everything in it clean and protected.
_____ 10. Don't vegetate; Participate!
_____ 11. Be the best welcoming committee a church ever had!

Weekly Scoring Section

Check the box of each meeting that you attend. The week starts on Sunday and ends on Saturday. For the Date _____ put the date of the Sunday that starts the week.

Sunday School .... 5,000 points
Sunday Morning .... 2,000 points
Sunday Night .... 4,000 points
Wednesday Night.. 5,000 points
Weekly Lightning Meeting.................................... 3,000 points
Nursing Home.. 5,000 points
Visitation.. 5,000 points
Revivals or Special Meetings .... 5,000 points
Bringing Book to Lightning Meeting .... 1,000 points

Week 1   Date _____
☐   Sunday School   ____   Bring Book to Meeting
☐   Sunday Morning   ☐   Nursing Home
☐   Sunday Night   ☐   Visitation
☐   Wednesday Night   ☐   Other (Specify)_____
☐   Lightning Meeting   ☐   Other (Specify)_____

Week 2   Date _____
☐   Sunday School   ____   Bring Book to Meeting
☐   Sunday Morning   ☐   Nursing Home
☐   Sunday Night   ☐   Visitation
☐   Wednesday Night   ☐   Other (Specify)_____
☐   Lightning Meeting   ☐   Other (Specify)_____

Week 3   Date _____
☐   Sunday School   ____   Bring Book to Meeting
☐   Sunday Morning   ☐   Nursing Home
☐   Sunday Night   ☐   Visitation
☐   Wednesday Night   ☐   Other (Specify)_____
☐   Lightning Meeting   ☐   Other (Specify)_____

Week 4   Date _____
☐   Sunday School   ____   Bring Book to Meeting
☐   Sunday Morning   ☐   Nursing Home
☐   Sunday Night   ☐   Visitation
☐   Wednesday Night   ☐   Other (Specify)_____
☐   Lightning Meeting   ☐   Other (Specify)_____

Week 5   Date _____
☐   Sunday School   ____   Bring Book to Meeting
☐   Sunday Morning   ☐   Nursing Home
☐   Sunday Night   ☐   Visitation
☐   Wednesday Night   ☐   Other (Specify)_____
☐   Lightning Meeting   ☐   Other (Specify)_____

Week 6   Date _____
☐   Sunday School   ____   Bring Book to Meeting
☐   Sunday Morning   ☐   Nursing Home
☐   Sunday Night   ☐   Visitation
☐   Wednesday Night   ☐   Other (Specify)_____
☐   Lightning Meeting   ☐   Other (Specify)_____

Week 7   Date _____
☐   Sunday School   ____   Bring Book to Meeting
☐   Sunday Morning   ☐   Nursing Home
☐   Sunday Night   ☐   Visitation
☐   Wednesday Night   ☐   Other (Specify)_____
☐   Lightning Meeting   ☐   Other (Specify)_____

Week 8   Date _____
☐   Sunday School   ____   Bring Book to Meeting
☐   Sunday Morning   ☐   Nursing Home
☐   Sunday Night   ☐   Visitation
☐   Wednesday Night   ☐   Other (Specify)_____
☐   Lightning Meeting   ☐   Other (Specify)_____

Week 9   Date _____
☐   Sunday School   ____   Bring Book to Meeting
☐   Sunday Morning   ☐   Nursing Home
☐   Sunday Night   ☐   Visitation
☐   Wednesday Night   ☐   Other (Specify)_____
☐   Lightning Meeting   ☐   Other (Specify)_____

Week 10   Date _____
☐   Sunday School   ____   Bring Book to Meeting
☐   Sunday Morning   ☐   Nursing Home
☐   Sunday Night   ☐   Visitation
☐   Wednesday Night   ☐   Other (Specify)_____
☐   Lightning Meeting   ☐   Other (Specify)_____

Week 11   Date _____
☐   Sunday School   ____ Bring Book to Meeting
☐   Sunday Morning   ☐   Nursing Home
☐   Sunday Night   ☐   Visitation
☐   Wednesday Night   ☐   Other (Specify)_____
☐   Lightning Meeting   ☐   Other (Specify)_____

Week 12   Date _____
☐   Sunday School   ____ Bring Book to Meeting
☐   Sunday Morning   ☐   Nursing Home
☐   Sunday Night   ☐   Visitation
☐   Wednesday Night   ☐   Other (Specify)_____
☐   Lightning Meeting   ☐   Other (Specify)_____

Week 13   Date _____
☐   Sunday School   ____ Bring Book to Meeting
☐   Sunday Morning   ☐   Nursing Home
☐   Sunday Night   ☐   Visitation
☐   Wednesday Night   ☐   Other (Specify)_____
☐   Lightning Meeting   ☐   Other (Specify)_____

Week 14   Date _____
☐   Sunday School   ____ Bring Book to Meeting
☐   Sunday Morning   ☐   Nursing Home
☐   Sunday Night   ☐   Visitation
☐   Wednesday Night   ☐   Other (Specify)_____
☐   Lightning Meeting   ☐   Other (Specify)_____

Week 15   Date _____
☐   Sunday School   ____   Bring Book to Meeting
☐   Sunday Morning   ☐   Nursing Home
☐   Sunday Night   ☐   Visitation
☐   Wednesday Night   ☐   Other (Specify)_____
☐   Lightning Meeting   ☐   Other (Specify)_____

Week 16   Date _____
☐   Sunday School   ____   Bring Book to Meeting
☐   Sunday Morning   ☐   Nursing Home
☐   Sunday Night   ☐   Visitation
☐   Wednesday Night   ☐   Other (Specify)_____
☐   Lightning Meeting   ☐   Other (Specify)_____

Week 17   Date _____
☐   Sunday School   ____   Bring Book to Meeting
☐   Sunday Morning   ☐   Nursing Home
☐   Sunday Night   ☐   Visitation
☐   Wednesday Night   ☐   Other (Specify)_____
☐   Lightning Meeting   ☐   Other (Specify)_____

Week 18   Date _____
☐   Sunday School   ____   Bring Book to Meeting
☐   Sunday Morning   ☐   Nursing Home
☐   Sunday Night   ☐   Visitation
☐   Wednesday Night   ☐   Other (Specify)_____
☐   Lightning Meeting   ☐   Other (Specify)_____

Week 19   Date _____
  ☐   Sunday School   ____ Bring Book to Meeting
  ☐   Sunday Morning   ☐ Nursing Home
  ☐   Sunday Night   ☐ Visitation
  ☐   Wednesday Night   ☐ Other (Specify)_____
  ☐   Lightning Meeting   ☐ Other (Specify)_____

Week 20   Date _____
  ☐   Sunday School   ____ Bring Book to Meeting
  ☐   Sunday Morning   ☐ Nursing Home
  ☐   Sunday Night   ☐ Visitation
  ☐   Wednesday Night   ☐ Other (Specify)_____
  ☐   Lightning Meeting   ☐ Other (Specify)_____

Week 21   Date _____
  ☐   Sunday School   ____ Bring Book to Meeting
  ☐   Sunday Morning   ☐ Nursing Home
  ☐   Sunday Night   ☐ Visitation
  ☐   Wednesday Night   ☐ Other (Specify)_____
  ☐   Lightning Meeting   ☐ Other (Specify)_____

Week 22   Date _____
  ☐   Sunday School   ____ Bring Book to Meeting
  ☐   Sunday Morning   ☐ Nursing Home
  ☐   Sunday Night   ☐ Visitation
  ☐   Wednesday Night   ☐ Other (Specify)_____
  ☐   Lightning Meeting   ☐ Other (Specify)_____

Week 23   Date _____
  ☐   Sunday School   ____   Bring Book to Meeting
  ☐   Sunday Morning   ☐   Nursing Home
  ☐   Sunday Night   ☐   Visitation
  ☐   Wednesday Night   ☐   Other (Specify)_____
  ☐   Lightning Meeting   ☐   Other (Specify)_____

Week 24   Date _____
  ☐   Sunday School   ____   Bring Book to Meeting
  ☐   Sunday Morning   ☐   Nursing Home
  ☐   Sunday Night   ☐   Visitation
  ☐   Wednesday Night   ☐   Other (Specify)_____
  ☐   Lightning Meeting   ☐   Other (Specify)_____

Week 25   Date _____
  ☐   Sunday School   ____   Bring Book to Meeting
  ☐   Sunday Morning   ☐   Nursing Home
  ☐   Sunday Night   ☐   Visitation
  ☐   Wednesday Night   ☐   Other (Specify)_____
  ☐   Lightning Meeting   ☐   Other (Specify)_____

Week 26   Date _____
  ☐   Sunday School   ____   Bring Book to Meeting
  ☐   Sunday Morning   ☐   Nursing Home
  ☐   Sunday Night   ☐   Visitation
  ☐   Wednesday Night   ☐   Other (Specify)_____
  ☐   Lightning Meeting   ☐   Other (Specify)_____

Week 27   Date _____
☐   Sunday School   ____   Bring Book to Meeting
☐   Sunday Morning   ☐   Nursing Home
☐   Sunday Night   ☐   Visitation
☐   Wednesday Night   ☐   Other (Specify)_____
☐   Lightning Meeting   ☐   Other (Specify)_____

Week 28   Date _____
☐   Sunday School   ____   Bring Book to Meeting
☐   Sunday Morning   ☐   Nursing Home
☐   Sunday Night   ☐   Visitation
☐   Wednesday Night   ☐   Other (Specify)_____
☐   Lightning Meeting   ☐   Other (Specify)_____

Week 29   Date _____
☐   Sunday School   ____   Bring Book to Meeting
☐   Sunday Morning   ☐   Nursing Home
☐   Sunday Night   ☐   Visitation
☐   Wednesday Night   ☐   Other (Specify)_____
☐   Lightning Meeting   ☐   Other (Specify)_____

Week 30   Date _____
☐   Sunday School   ____   Bring Book to Meeting
☐   Sunday Morning   ☐   Nursing Home
☐   Sunday Night   ☐   Visitation
☐   Wednesday Night   ☐   Other (Specify)_____
☐   Lightning Meeting   ☐   Other (Specify)_____

Week 31   Date _____
☐   Sunday School   ____ Bring Book to Meeting
☐   Sunday Morning   ☐   Nursing Home
☐   Sunday Night   ☐   Visitation
☐   Wednesday Night   ☐   Other (Specify)_____
☐   Lightning Meeting   ☐   Other (Specify)_____

Week 32   Date _____
☐   Sunday School   ____ Bring Book to Meeting
☐   Sunday Morning   ☐   Nursing Home
☐   Sunday Night   ☐   Visitation
☐   Wednesday Night   ☐   Other (Specify)_____
☐   Lightning Meeting   ☐   Other (Specify)_____

Week 33   Date _____
☐   Sunday School   ____ Bring Book to Meeting
☐   Sunday Morning   ☐   Nursing Home
☐   Sunday Night   ☐   Visitation
☐   Wednesday Night   ☐   Other (Specify)_____
☐   Lightning Meeting   ☐   Other (Specify)_____

Week 34   Date _____
☐   Sunday School   ____ Bring Book to Meeting
☐   Sunday Morning   ☐   Nursing Home
☐   Sunday Night   ☐   Visitation
☐   Wednesday Night   ☐   Other (Specify)_____
☐   Lightning Meeting   ☐   Other (Specify)_____

Visitors

Each person you bring to church you can count as a visitor.
You can count each person up to three times.

Visitors. . . . . 5,000 points

Name	1st	2nd	3rd
_____	_____	_____	_____
_____	_____	_____	_____
_____	_____	_____	_____
_____	_____	_____	_____
_____	_____	_____	_____
_____	_____	_____	_____
_____	_____	_____	_____
_____	_____	_____	_____
_____	_____	_____	_____
_____	_____	_____	_____
_____	_____	_____	_____
_____	_____	_____	_____
_____	_____	_____	_____

Special Scoring Section

This year you will be given the opportunity to earn points for special activities, games, and trivia. Use this page to write down the activities that you complete and have your sponsor initial that you did complete it along with the points that are associated with the activity.

_____
_____
_____
_____
_____
_____
_____
_____
_____
_____
_____
_____
_____
_____
_____
_____
_____
_____
_____
_____
_____
_____
_____
_____
_____
_____

Book Reading List

The books below can be read and a one page summary can be
turned in for the specified points below. Have your sponsor
initial once the report has been turned in.

_____   Pilgrims Progress by John Bunyon. 15,000

_____   The Hiding Place by Corrie Ten Boom 15,000

_____   The Lion, the Witch, and the Wardrobe by C. S. Lewis
. 7,000

_____   In His Steps by Charles M. Sheldon 15,000

_____   The Pursuit of God by A. W. Tozer 15,000

_____   Power Through Prayer by E.M Bounds 15,000

Other books that your Youth Leader specifies that you may
read this year.

_____   _____
_____   _____
_____   _____
_____   _____
_____   _____
_____   _____
_____   _____
_____   _____
_____   _____
_____   _____
_____   _____
_____   _____
_____   _____
_____   _____
_____   _____
_____   _____
_____   _____

Bible Reading Section

Each chapter is worth 500 points. You must read it and give a one line summary of it. It must be in your own words, not what some Bible has as a chapter heading.

If you finish the whole Bible in 34 weeks you will get a bonus of 405,500 points bringing your total for reading the Bible to 1,000,000 points.

Example:

Hezekiah 1   <u>The sin of Hezekiah, eating his brother's pizza without permission</u>.

Genesis 1   _____
             _____

Genesis 2   _____
             _____

Genesis 3   _____
             _____

Genesis 4   _____
             _____

Genesis 5   _____
             _____

Genesis 6   _____
             _____

Genesis 7   _____
             _____

Genesis 8   _____
             _____

Genesis 9   _____
             _____

Genesis 10   _____
             _____

Genesis 11 _____

Genesis 12 _____

Genesis 13 _____

Genesis 14 _____

Genesis 15 _____

Genesis 16 _____

Genesis 17 _____

Genesis 18 _____

Genesis 19 _____

Genesis 20 _____

Genesis 21 _____

Genesis 22 _____

Genesis 23 _____

Genesis 24 _____

Genesis 25 _____

Genesis 26 _____

Genesis 27 _____

Genesis 28 _____

Genesis 29 _____

Genesis 30 _____

Genesis 31 _____

Genesis 32 _____

Genesis 33 _____

Genesis 34 _____

Genesis 35 _____

Genesis 36 _____

Genesis 37 _____

Genesis 38 _____

Genesis 39 _____

Genesis 40 _____

Genesis 41 _____

Genesis 42 _____

Genesis 43 _____

Genesis 44 _____

Genesis 45 _____

Genesis 46 _____

Genesis 47 _____

Genesis 48 _____

Genesis 49 _____

Genesis 50 _____

Exodus 1 _____

Exodus 2 _____

Exodus 3 _____

Exodus 4 _____

Exodus 5 _____

Exodus 6 _____

Exodus 7 _____

Exodus 8 _____

Exodus 9 _____

Exodus 10 _____

Exodus 11 _____

Exodus 12 _____

Exodus 13 _____

Exodus 14 _____

Exodus 15 _____

Exodus 16 _____

Exodus 17 _____

Exodus 18 _____

Exodus 19 _____

Exodus 20 _____

Exodus 21 _____

Exodus 22 _____

Exodus 23 _____

Exodus 24 _____

Exodus 25 _____

Exodus 26 _____

Exodus 27 _____

Exodus 28 _____

Exodus 29 _____

Exodus 30 _____

Exodus 31 _____

Exodus 32 _____

Exodus 33 _____

Exodus 34 _____

Exodus 35 _____

Exodus 36 _____

Exodus 37 _____

Exodus 38 _____

Exodus 39 _____

Exodus 40 _____

Leviticus 1 _____

Leviticus 2 _____

Leviticus 3 _____

Leviticus 4 _____

Leviticus 5 _____

Leviticus 6 _____

Leviticus 7 _____

Leviticus 8 _____

Leviticus 9 _____

Leviticus 10 _____

Leviticus 11 _____

Leviticus 12 _____

Leviticus 13 _____

Leviticus 14 _____

Leviticus 15 _____

Leviticus 16 _____

Leviticus 17 _____

Leviticus 18 _____

Leviticus 19 _____

Leviticus 20 _____

Leviticus 21 _____

Leviticus 22 _____

Leviticus 23 _____

Leviticus 24 _____

Leviticus 25 _____

Leviticus 26 _____

Leviticus 27 _____

Numbers 1 _____

Numbers 2 _____

Numbers 3 _____

Numbers 4 _____

Numbers 5 _____

Numbers 6 _____

Numbers 7 _____

Numbers 8 _____

Numbers 9 _____

Numbers 10 _____

Numbers 11 _____

Numbers 12 _____

Numbers 13 _____

Numbers 14 _____

Numbers 15 _____

Numbers 16 _____

Numbers 17 _____

Numbers 18 _____

Numbers 19 _____

Numbers 20 _____

Numbers 21 _____

Numbers 22 _____

Numbers 23 _____

Numbers 24 _____

Numbers 25 _____

Numbers 26 _____

Numbers 27 _____

Numbers 28 _____

Numbers 29 _____

Numbers 30 _____

Numbers 31 _____

Numbers 32 _____

Numbers 33 _____

Numbers 34 _____

Numbers 35 _____

Numbers 36 _____

Deut. 1 _____

Deut. 2 _____

Deut. 3 _____

Deut. 4 _____

Deut. 5 _____

Deut. 6 _____

Deut. 7 _____

Deut. 8 _____

Deut. 9 _____

Deut. 10 _____

Deut. 11 _____

Deut. 12 _____

Deut. 13 _____

Deut. 14 _____

Deut. 15 _____

Deut. 16 _____

Deut. 17 _____

Deut. 18 _____

Deut. 19 _____

Deut. 20 _____

Deut. 21 _____

Deut. 22 _____

Deut. 23 _____

Deut. 24 _____

Deut. 25 _____

Deut. 26 _____

Dcut. 27 _____

Deut 28 _____

Deut. 29 _____

Deut. 30 _____

Deut. 31 _____

Deut. 32 _____

Deut. 33 _____

Deut. 34 _____

Joshua 1 _____

Joshua 2 _____

Joshua 3 _____

Joshua 4 _____

Joshua 5 _____

Joshua 6 _____

Joshua 7 _____

Joshua 8 _____

Joshua 9 _____

Joshua 10 _____
_____

Joshua 11 _____
_____

Joshua 12 _____
_____

Joshua 13 _____
_____

Joshua 14 _____
_____

Joshua 15 _____
_____

Joshua 16 _____
_____

Joshua 17 _____
_____

Joshua 18 _____
_____

Joshua 19 _____
_____

Joshua 20 _____
_____

Joshua 21 _____
_____

Joshua 22 _____
_____

Joshua 23 _____
_____

Joshua 24 _____
_____

Judges 1 _____
_____

Judges 2 _____
_____

Judges 3 _____
_____

Judges 4 _____

Judges 5 _____

Judges 6 _____

Judges 7 _____

Judges 8 _____

Judges 9 _____

Judges 10 _____

Judges 11 _____

Judges 12 _____

Judges 13 _____

Judges 14 _____

Judges 15 _____

Judges 16 _____

Judges 17 _____

Judges 18 _____

Judges 19 _____

Judges 20 _____

Judges 21 _____

Ruth 1 _____

Ruth 2 _____

Ruth 3 _____

Ruth 4 _____

1 Samuel 1 _____

1 Samuel 2 _____

1 Samuel 3 _____

1 Samuel 4 _____

1 Samuel 5 _____

1 Samuel 6 _____

1 Samuel 7 _____

1 Samuel 8 _____

1 Samuel 9 _____

1 Samuel 10 _____

1 Samuel 11 _____

1 Samuel 12 _____

1 Samuel 13 _____

1 Samuel 14 _____

1 Samuel 15 _____

1 Samuel 16

1 Samuel 17

1 Samuel 18

1 Samuel 19

1 Samuel 20

1 Samuel 21

1 Samuel 22

1 Samuel 23

1 Samuel 24

1 Samuel 25

1 Samuel 26

1 Samuel 27

1 Samuel 28

1 Samuel 29

1 Samuel 30

1 Samuel 31

2 Samuel 1

2 Samuel 2

2 Samuel 3 _____

2 Samuel 4 _____

2 Samuel 5 _____

2 Samuel 6 _____

2 Samuel 7 _____

2 Samuel 8 _____

2 Samuel 9 _____

2 Samuel 10 _____

2 Samuel 11 _____

2 Samuel 12 _____

2 Samuel 13 _____

2 Samuel 14 _____

2 Samuel 15 _____

2 Samuel 16 _____

2 Samuel 17 _____

2 Samuel 18 _____

2 Samuel 19 _____

2 Samuel 20 _____

2 Samuel 21 _____

2 Samuel 22 _____

2 Samuel 23 _____

2 Samuel 24 _____

1 Kings 1 _____

1 Kings 2 _____

1 Kings 3 _____

1 Kings 4 _____

1 Kings 5 _____

1 Kings 6 _____

1 Kings 7 _____

1 Kings 8 _____

1 Kings 9 _____

1 Kings 10 _____

1 Kings 11 _____

1 Kings 12 _____

1 Kings 13 _____

1 Kings 14 _____

1 Kings 15 _____

1 Kings 16 _____

1 Kings 17 _____

1 Kings 18 _____

1 Kings 19 _____

1 Kings 20 _____

1 Kings 21 _____

1 Kings 22 _____

2 Kings 1 _____

2 Kings 2 _____

2 Kings 3 _____

2 Kings 4 _____

2 Kings 5 _____

2 Kings 6 _____

2 Kings 7 _____

2 Kings 8 _____

2 Kings 9 _____

2 Kings 10 _____

2 Kings 11 _____

2 Kings 12 _____

2 Kings 13 _____

2 Kings 14 _____

2 Kings 15 _____

2 Kings 16 _____

2 Kings 17 _____

2 Kings 18 _____

2 Kings 19 _____

2 Kings 20 _____

2 Kings 21 _____

2 Kings 22 _____

2 Kings 23 _____

2 Kings 24 _____

2 Kings 25 _____

1 Chron. 1 _____

1 Chron. 2 _____

1 Chron. 3 _____

1 Chron. 4 _____

1 Chron. 5 _____

1 Chron. 6 _____

1 Chron. 7 _____

1 Chron. 8 _____

1 Chron. 9 _____

1 Chron. 10 _____

1 Chron. 11 _____

1 Chron. 12 _____

1 Chron. 13 _____

1 Chron. 14 _____

1 Chron. 15 _____

1 Chron. 16 _____

1 Chron. 17 _____

1 Chron. 18 _____

1 Chron. 19 _____

1 Chron. 20 _____

1 Chron. 21 _____

1 Chron. 22 _____

1 Chron. 23 _____

1 Chron. 24 _____

1 Chron. 25 _____

1 Chron. 26 _____

1 Chron. 27 _____

1 Chron. 28 _____

1 Chron. 29 _____

2 Chron. 1 _____

2 Chron. 2 _____

2 Chron. 3 _____

2 Chron. 4 _____

2 Chron. 5 _____

2 Chron. 6 _____

2 Chron. 7 _____

2 Chron. 8 _____

2 Chron. 9 _____

2 Chron. 10 _____

2 Chron. 11 _____

2 Chron. 12 _____

2 Chron. 13 _____

2 Chron. 14 _____

2 Chron. 15 _____

2 Chron. 16 _____

2 Chron. 17 _____

2 Chron. 18 _____

2 Chron. 19 _____

2 Chron. 20 _____

2 Chron. 21 _____

2 Chron. 22 _____

2 Chron. 23 _____

2 Chron. 24 _____

2 Chron. 25 _____

2 Chron. 26 _____

2 Chron. 27 _____

2 Chron. 28 _____

2 Chron. 29 _____

2 Chron. 30 _____

2 Chron. 31 _____

2 Chron. 32 _____

2 Chron. 33	_____
2 Chron. 34	_____
2 Chron. 35	_____
2 Chron. 36	_____
Ezra 1	_____
Ezra 2	_____
Ezra 3	_____
Ezra 4	_____
Ezra 5	_____
Ezra 6	_____
Ezra 7	_____
Ezra 8	_____
Ezra 9	_____
Ezra 10	_____
Nehemiah 1	_____
Nehemiah 2	_____
Nehemiah 3	_____
Nehemiah 4	_____

Nehemiah 5 _____

Nehemiah 6 _____

Nehemiah 7 _____

Nehemiah 8 _____

Nehemiah 9 _____

Nehemiah 10 _____

Nehemiah 11 _____

Nehemiah 12 _____

Nehemiah 13 _____

Esther 1 _____

Esther 2 _____

Esther 3 _____

Esther 4 _____

Esther 5 _____

Esther 6 _____

Esther 7 _____

Esther 8 _____

Esther 9 _____

Esther 10 _____

Job 1 _____

Job 2 _____

Job 3 _____

Job 4 _____

Job 5 _____

Job 6 _____

Job 7 _____

Job 8 _____

Job 9 _____

Job 10 _____

Job 11 _____

Job 12 _____

Job 13 _____

Job 14 _____

Job 15 _____

Job 16 _____

Job 17 _____

Job 18 _____

Job 19 _____

Job 20 _____

Job 21 _____

Job 22 _____

Job 23 _____

Job 24 _____

Job 25 _____

Job 26 _____

Job 27 _____

Job 28 _____

Job 29 _____

Job 30 _____

Job 31 _____

Job 32 _____

Job 33 _____

Job 34 _____

Job 35 _____

Job 36 _____

Job 37 _____

Job 38 _____

Job 39 _____

Job 40 _____

Job 41 _____

Job 42 _____

Psalm 1 _____

Psalm 2 _____

Psalm 3 _____

Psalm 4 _____

Psalm 5 _____

Psalm 6 _____

Psalm 7 _____

Psalm 8 _____

Psalm 9 _____

Psalm 10 _____

Psalm 11 _____

Psalm 12 _____

Psalm 13 _____

Psalm 14   _____

Psalm 15   _____

Psalm 16   _____

Psalm 17   _____

Psalm 18   _____

Psalm 19   _____

Psalm 20   _____

Psalm 21   _____

Psalm 22   _____

Psalm 23   _____

Psalm 24   _____

Psalm 25   _____

Psalm 26   _____

Psalm 27   _____

Psalm 28   _____

Psalm 29   _____

Psalm 30   _____

Psalm 31   _____

Psalm 32   _____

Psalm 33 _____

Psalm 34 _____

Psalm 35 _____

Psalm 36 _____

Psalm 37 _____

Psalm 38 _____

Psalm 39 _____

Psalm 40 _____

Psalm 41 _____

Psalm 42 _____

Psalm 43 _____

Psalm 44 _____

Psalm 45 _____

Psalm 46 _____

Psalm 47 _____

Psalm 48 _____

Psalm 49 _____

Psalm 50 _____

Psalm 51 _____

Psalm 52 _____

Psalm 53 _____

Psalm 54 _____

Psalm 55 _____

Psalm 56 _____

Psalm 57 _____

Psalm 58 _____

Psalm 59 _____

Psalm 60 _____

Psalm 61 _____

Psalm 62 _____

Psalm 63 _____

Psalm 64 _____

Psalm 65 _____

Psalm 66 _____

Psalm 67 _____

Psalm 68 _____

Psalm 69 _____

Psalm 70 _____

Psalm 71 _____

Psalm 72 _____

Psalm 73 _____

Psalm 74 _____

Psalm 75 _____

Psalm 76 _____

Psalm 77 _____

Psalm 78 _____

Psalm 79 _____

Psalm 80 _____

Psalm 81 _____

Psalm 82 _____

Psalm 83 _____

Psalm 84 _____

Psalm 85 _____

Psalm 86 _____

Psalm 87 _____

Psalm 88 _____

Psalm 89 _____

Psalm 90 _____

Psalm 91 _____

Psalm 92 _____

Psalm 93 _____

Psalm 94 _____

Psalm 95 _____

Psalm 96 _____

Psalm 97 _____

Psalm 98 _____

Psalm 99 _____

Psalm 100 _____

Psalm 101 _____

Psalm 102 _____

Psalm 103 _____

Psalm 104 _____

Psalm 105 _____

Psalm 106 _____

Psalm 107 _____

Psalm 108 _____

Psalm 109 _____

Psalm 110 _____

Psalm 111 _____

Psalm 112 _____

Psalm 113 _____

Psalm 114 _____

Psalm 115 _____

Psalm 116 _____

Psalm 117 _____

Psalm 118 _____

Psalm 119 _____

Psalm 120 _____

Psalm 121 _____

Psalm 122 _____

Psalm 123 _____

Psalm 124 _____

Psalm 125 _____

Psalm 126 _____

Psalm 127 _____

Psalm 128 _____

Psalm 129 _____

Psalm 130 _____

Psalm 131 _____

Psalm 132 _____

Psalm 133 _____

Psalm 134 _____

Psalm 135 _____

Psalm 136 _____

Psalm 137 _____

Psalm 138 _____

Psalm 139 _____

Psalm 140 _____

Psalm 141 _____

Psalm 142 _____

Psalm 143 _____

Psalm 144 _____

Psalm 145 _____

Psalm 146 _____

Psalm 147 _____

Psalm 148 _____

Psalm 149 _____

Psalm 150 _____

Proverbs 1 _____

Proverbs 2 _____

Proverbs 3 _____

Proverbs 4 _____

Proverbs 5 _____

Proverbs 6 _____

Proverbs 7 _____

Proverbs 8 _____

Proverbs 9 _____

Proverbs 10 _____

Proverbs 11 _____

Proverbs 12 _____

Proverbs 13 _____

Proverbs 14 _____

Proverbs 15 _____

Proverbs 16 _____

Proverbs 17 _____

Proverbs 18 _____

Proverbs 19 _____

Proverbs 20 _____

Proverbs 21 _____

Proverbs 22 _____

Proverbs 23 _____

Proverbs 24 _____

Proverbs 25 _____

Proverbs 26 _____

Proverbs 27 _____

Proverbs 28 _____

Proverbs 29 _____

Proverbs 30 _____

Proverbs 31 _____

Eccles. 1 _____

Eccles. 2 _____

Eccles. 3 _____

Eccles. 4 _____

Eccles. 5 _____

Eccles. 6 _____

Eccles. 7 _____

Eccles. 8 _____

Eccles. 9 _____

Eccles. 10 _____

Eccles. 11 _____

Eccles. 12 _____

Song of Sol. 1 _____

Song of Sol. 2 _____

Song of Sol. 3 _____

Song of Sol. 4 _____

Song of Sol. 5 _____

Song of Sol. 6 _____

Song of Sol. 7 _____

Song of Sol. 8 _____

Isaiah 1 _____

Isaiah 2 _____

Isaiah 3 _____

Isaiah 4 _____

Isaiah 5 _____

Isaiah 6 _____

Isaiah 7 _____

Isaiah 8 _____

Isaiah 9 _____

Isaiah 10 _____

Isaiah 11 _____

Isaiah 12 _____

Isaiah 13 _____

Isaiah 14 _____

Isaiah 15 _____

Isaiah 16 _____

Isaiah 17 _____

Isaiah 18 _____

Isaiah 19 _____

Isaiah 20 _____

Isaiah 21 _____

Isaiah 22 _____

Isaiah 23 _____

Isaiah 24 _____

Isaiah 25 _____

Isaiah 26 _____

Isaiah 27 _____

Isaiah 28 _____

Isaiah 29 _____

Isaiah 30 _____

Isaiah 31 _____

Isaiah 32 _____

Isaiah 33 _____

Isaiah 34 _____

Isaiah 35 _____

Isaiah 36 _____

Isaiah 37 _____

Isaiah 38 _____

Isaiah 39 _____

Isaiah 40 _____

Isaiah 41 _____

Isaiah 42 _____

Isaiah 43 _____

Isaiah 44 _____

Isaiah 45 _____

Isaiah 46 _____

Isaiah 47 _____

Isaiah 48 _____

Isaiah 49 _____

Isaiah 50 _____

Isaiah 51 _____

Isaiah 52 _____

Isaiah 53 _____

Isaiah 54 _____

Isaiah 55 _____

Isaiah 56 _____

Isaiah 57 _____

Isaiah 58 _____

Isaiah 59 _____

Isaiah 60 _____

Isaiah 61 _____

Isaiah 62 _____

Isaiah 63 _____

Isaiah 64 _____

Isaiah 65 _____

Isaiah 66 _____

Jeremiah 1 _____

Jeremiah 2 _____

Jeremiah 3 _____

Jeremiah 4 _____

Jeremiah 5 _____

Jeremiah 6 _____

Jeremiah 7 _____

Jeremiah 8 _____

Jeremiah 9 _____

Jeremiah 10 _____

Jeremiah 11 _____

Jeremiah 12 _____

Jeremiah 13 _____

Jeremiah 14 _____

Jeremiah 15 _____

Jeremiah 16 _____

Jeremiah 17 _____

Jeremiah 18 _____

Jeremiah 19 _____

Jeremiah 20 _____

Jeremiah 21 _____

Jeremiah 22 _____

Jeremiah 23 _____

Jeremiah 24 _____

Jeremiah 25 _____

Jeremiah 26 _____

Jeremiah 27 _____

Jeremiah 28 _____

Jeremiah 29 _____

Jeremiah 30 _____

Jeremiah 31 _____

Jeremiah 32 _____

Jeremiah 33 _____

Jeremiah 34 _____

Jeremiah 35 _____

Jeremiah 36 _____

Jeremiah 37 _____

Jeremiah 38 _____

Jeremiah 39 _____

Jeremiah 40 _____

Jeremiah 41 _____

Jeremiah 42 _____

Jeremiah 43 _____

Jeremiah 44 _____

Jeremiah 45 _____

Jeremiah 46 _____

Jeremiah 47 _____

Jeremiah 48 _____

Jeremiah 49 _____

Jeremiah 50 _____

Jeremiah 51 _____

Jeremiah 52 _____

Lament. 1 _____

Lament. 2 _____

Lament. 3 _____

Lament. 4 _____

Lament. 5 _____

Ezekiel 1 _____

Ezekiel 2 _____

Ezekiel 3 _____

Ezekiel 4 _____

Ezekiel 5 _____

Ezekiel 6 _____

Ezekiel 7 _____

Ezekiel 8 _____

Ezekiel 9 _____

Ezekiel 10 _____

Ezekiel 11 _____

Ezekiel 12 _____

Ezekiel 13 _____

Ezekiel 14 _____

Ezekiel 15 _____

Ezekiel 16 _____

Ezekiel 17 _____

Ezekiel 18 _____

Ezekiel 19 _____

Ezekiel 20 _____

Ezekiel 21 _____

Ezekiel 22 _____

Ezekiel 23 _____

Ezekiel 24 _____

Ezekiel 25 _____

Ezekiel 26 _____

Ezekiel 27 _____

Ezekiel 28 _____

Ezekiel 29 _____

Ezekiel 30 _____

Ezekiel 31 _____

Ezekiel 32 _____

Ezekiel 33 _____

Ezekiel 34 _____

Ezekiel 35 _____

Ezekiel 36 _____

Ezekiel 37 _____

Ezekiel 38 _____

Ezekiel 39 _____

Ezekiel 40 _____

Ezekiel 41 _____

Ezekiel 42 _____

Ezekiel 43 _____

Ezekiel 44 _____

Ezekiel 45 _____

Ezekiel 46 _____

Ezekiel 47 _____

Ezekiel 48 _____

Daniel 1 _____

Daniel 2 _____

Daniel 3 _____

Daniel 4 _____

Daniel 5 _____

Daniel 6 _____

Daniel 7 _____

Daniel 8 _____

Daniel 9 _____

Daniel 10 _____

Daniel 11 _____

Daniel 12 _____

Hosea 1 _____

Hosea 2 _____

Hosea 3 _____

Hosea 4 _____

Hosea 5 _____

Hosea 6 _____

Hosea 7 _____

Hosea 8 _____

Hosea 9 _____

Hosea 10 _____

Hosea 11 _____

Hosea 12 _____

Hosea 13 _____

Hosea 14 _____

Joel 1 _____

Joel 2 _____

Joel 3 _____

Amos 1 _____

Amos 2 _____

Amos 3 _____

Amos 4 _____

Amos 5 _____

Amos 6 _____

Amos 7 _____

Amos 8 _____

Amos 9 _____

Obadiah 1 _____

Jonah 1 _____

Jonah 2 _____

Jonah 3 _____

Jonah 4 _____

Micah 1 _____

Micah 2 _____

Micah 3 _____

Micah 4 _____

Micah 5 _____

Micah 6 _____

Micah 7 _____

Nahum 1 _____

Nahum 2 _____

Nahum 3 _____

Habakkuk 1 _____

Habakkuk 2 _____

Habakkuk 3 _____

Zephaniah 1 _____

Zephaniah 2 _____

Zephaniah 3 _____

Haggai 1 _____

Haggai 2 _____

Zechariah 1 _____

Zechariah 2 _____

Zechariah 3 _____

Zechariah 4 _____

Zechariah 5 _____

Zechariah 6 _____

Zechariah 7 _____

Zechariah 8 _____

Zechariah 9 _____

Zechariah 10 _____

Zechariah 11 _____

Zechariah 12 _____

Zechariah 13 _____

Zechariah 14 _____

Malachi 1 _____

Malachi 2 _____

Malachi 3 _____

Malachi 4 _____

Matthew 1 _____

Matthew 2 _____

Matthew 3 _____

Matthew 4 _____

Matthew 5 _____

Matthew 6 _____

Matthew 7 _____

Matthew 8 _____

Matthew 9 _____

Matthew 10 _____

Matthew 11 _____

Matthew 12 _____

Matthew 13 _____

Matthew 14 _____

Matthew 15 _____

Matthew 16 _____

Matthew 17 _____

Matthew 18 _____

Matthew 19 _____

Matthew 20 _____

Matthew 21 _____

Matthew 22 _____

Matthew 23 _____

Matthew 24 _____

Matthew 25 _____

Matthew 26 _____

Matthew 27 _____

Matthew 28 _____

Mark 1 _____

Mark 2 _____

Mark 3 _____

Mark 4 _____

Mark 5 _____

Mark 6 _____

Mark 7 _____

Mark 8 _____

Mark 9 _____

Mark 10 _____

Mark 11 _____

Mark 12 _____

Mark 13 _____

Mark 14 _____

Mark 15 _____

Mark 16 _____

Luke 1 _____

Luke 2 _____

Luke 3 _____

Luke 4 _____

Luke 5 _____

Luke 6 _____

Luke 7 _____

Luke 8 _____

Luke 9 _____

Luke 10 _____

Luke 11 _____

Luke 12 _____

Luke 13 _____

Luke 14 _____

Luke 15 _____

Luke 16 _____

Luke 17 _____

Luke 18 _____

Luke 19 _____

Luke 20 _____

Luke 21 _____

Luke 22 _____

Luke 23 _____

Luke 24 _____

John 1 _____

John 2 _____

John 3 _____

John 4 _____

John 5 _____

John 6 _____

John 7 _____

John 8 _____

John 9 _____

John 10 _____

John 11 _____

John 12 _____

John 13 _____

John 14 _____

John 15 _____

John 16 _____

John 17 _____

John 18 _____

John 19 _____

John 20 _____

John 21 _____

Acts 1 _____

Acts 2 _____

Acts 3 _____

Acts 4 _____

Acts 5 _____

Acts 6 _____

Acts 7 _____

Acts 8 _____

Acts 9 _____

Acts 10 _____

Acts 11 _____

Acts 12 _____

Acts 13 _____

Acts 14 _____

Acts 15 _____

Acts 16 _____

Acts 17 _____

Acts 18 _____

Acts 19 _____

Acts 20 _____

Acts 21 _____

Acts 22 _____

Acts 23 _____

Acts 24 _____

Acts 25 _____

Acts 26 _____

Acts 27 _____

Acts 28 _____

Romans 1 _____

Romans 2 _____

Romans 3 _____

Romans 4 _____

Romans 5 _____

Romans 6 _____

Romans 7 _____

Romans 8 _____

Romans 9 _____

Romans 10 _____

Romans 11 _____

Romans 12 _____

Romans 13 _____

Romans 14 _____

Romans 15 _____

Romans 16 _____

1 Corinth. 1 _____

1 Corinth. 2 _____

1 Corinth. 3 _____

1 Corinth. 4 _____

1 Corinth. 5 _____

1 Corinth. 6 _____

1 Corinth. 7 _____

1 Corinth. 8 _____

1 Corinth. 9 _____

1 Corinth. 10 _____

1 Corinth. 11 _____

1 Corinth. 12 _____

1 Corinth. 13 _____

1 Corinth. 14 _____

1 Corinth. 15 _____

1 Corinth. 16 _____

2 Corinth. 1 _____

2 Corinth. 2 _____

2 Corinth. 3 _____

2 Corinth. 4 _____

2 Corinth. 5 _____

2 Corinth. 6 _____

2 Corinth. 7 _____

2 Corinth. 8 _____

2 Corinth. 9 _____

2 Corinth. 10 _____

2 Corinth. 11 _____

2 Corinth. 12 _____

2 Corinth. 13 _____

Galatians 1 _____

Galatians 2 _____

Galatians 3 _____

Galatians 4 _____

Galatians 5 _____

Galatians 6 _____

Ephesians 1 _____

Ephesians 2 _____

Ephesians 3 _____

Ephesians 4 _____

Ephesians 5 _____

Ephesians 6 _____

Philippians 1 _____

Philippians 2 _____

Philippians 3 _____

Philippians 4 _____

Colossians 1 _____

Colossians 2 _____

Colossians 3 _____

Colossians 4 _____

1 Thess. 1 _____

1 Thess. 2 _____

1 Thess. 3 _____

1 Thess. 4 _____

1 Thess. 5 _____

2 Thess. 1 _____

2 Thess. 2 _____

2 Thess. 3 _____

1 Timothy 1 _____

1 Timothy 2 _____

1 Timothy 3 _____

1 Timothy 4 _____

1 Timothy 5 _____

1 Timothy 6 _____

2 Timothy 1 _____

2 Timothy 2 _____

2 Timothy 3 _____

2 Timothy 4 _____

Titus 1 _____

Titus 2 _____

Titus 3 _____

Philemon 1 _____

Hebrews 1 _____

Hebrews 2 _____

Hebrews 3 _____

Hebrews 4 _____

Hebrews 5 _____

Hebrews 6 _____

Hebrews 7 _____

Hebrews 8 _____

Hebrews 9 _____

Hebrews 10 _____

Hebrews 11 _____

Hebrews 12 _____

Hebrews 13 _____

James 1 _____

James 2 _____

James 3 _____

James 4 _____

James 5 _____

1 Peter 1 _____

1 Peter 2 _____

1 Peter 3 _____

1 Peter 4 _____

1 Peter 5 _____

2 Peter 1 _____

2 Peter 2 _____

2 Peter 3 _____

1 John 1 _____

1 John 2 _____

1 John 3 _____

1 John 4 _____

1 John 5 _____

2 John 1 _____

3 John 1 _____

Jude 1 _____

Revelation 1 _____

Revelation 2 _____

Revelation 3 _____

Revelation 4 _____

Revelation 5 _____

Revelation 6 _____

Revelation 7 _____

Revelation 8 _____

Revelation 9 _____

Revelation 10 _____

Revelation 11 _____

Revelation 12 _____

Revelation 13 _____

Revelation 14 _____

Revelation 15 _____

Revelation 16 _____

Revelation 17 _____

Revelation 18 _____

Revelation 19 _____

Revelation 20 _____

Revelation 21 _____

Revelation 22 _____

_____ Bonus for Whole Bible . . . . 405,500 points

Awards

The Mary Award.................................... Female Submissive Spirit
The Abraham Award ....Male Submissive Spirit
The Deborah Award ....Female Leadership
The Joshua Award .... Male Leadership
The Daniel Award..............................Steadfastness (Consistency)
The Peter Award .... Most Christian Growth
The Andrew Award .... Most Visitors
The Psalm 119:11 Award .... Most Verses Said
The Philippians 3:14 Award .... Most Points
The Philippians 2:5-8 Award............................... Most Christ-like

www.ingramcontent.com/pod-product-compliance
Lightning Source LLC
Chambersburg PA
CBHW071609040426
42452CB00008B/1295